Look and Learn

A First Book about

Bodies

The original publishers would like to thank the following
children and their parents for modeling for this book:
Joshua Ayshford, Karl and Lee Bolger, Francesca and Martina Brighton,
Caspian Broad, Andrew Brown, April Cain, Tayah Ettienne, Matthew Ferguson,
Safari George, Zoe Harrison, Alice and Kathleen Jenkins (and mother Louise),
Nicholas Lie, Houw Mau, Amber McLaren, Rebekah Murrell,
Olivia Pearce, Giovanni and Giuseppe Sipiano.

**For a free color catalog describing Gareth Stevens
Publishing's list of high-quality books and multimedia
programs, call 1-800-542-2595 (USA) or 1-800-461-9120
(Canada). Gareth Stevens Publishing's Fax: (414) 225-0377.**

Library of Congress Cataloging-in-Publication Data

Tuxworth, Nicola.
    A first book about bodies / by Nicola Tuxworth.
      p. cm. — (Look and learn)
    Includes bibliographical references and index.
    Summary: Photographs and simple text introduce different
parts of the body, how they work, and how they are used.
    ISBN 0-8368-2286-2 (lib. bdg.)
    1. Body, Human—Juvenile literature. 2. Human anatomy—
Juvenile literature. [1. Body, Human. 2. Human anatomy.]
I. Title. II. Series: Tuxworth, Nicola. Look and learn.
QM27.T89 1999
611—dc21   98-31772

This North American edition first published in 1999 by
Gareth Stevens Publishing
1555 North RiverCenter Drive, Suite 201
Milwaukee, WI 53212 USA

Original edition © 1996 by Anness Publishing Limited.
First published in 1996 by Lorenz Books, an imprint
of Anness Publishing Inc., New York, New York.
This U.S. edition © 1999 by Gareth Stevens, Inc.
Additional end matter © 1999 by Gareth Stevens, Inc.

Senior editor: Sue Grabham
Editor: Sophie Warne
Photographer: Lucy Tizard
Design and Typesetting: Michael Leaman Design Partnership
Illustrators: Marion Elliot and Alisa Tingley

Picture credits: Aquila/Hanne and Jens Eriksen: pp. 20t, 21m;
P. C. Howard: p. 21b; Bruce Coleman Ltd/John Visser: p. 20b;
Zefa: p. 13mr.

Printed in Mexico

1 2 3 4 5 6 7 8 9 03 02 01 00 99

Look and Learn

A First Book about
Bodies

Nicola Tuxworth

Gareth Stevens Publishing
MILWAUKEE

Your Body

Your body has lots of different parts. Each part helps you do certain things.

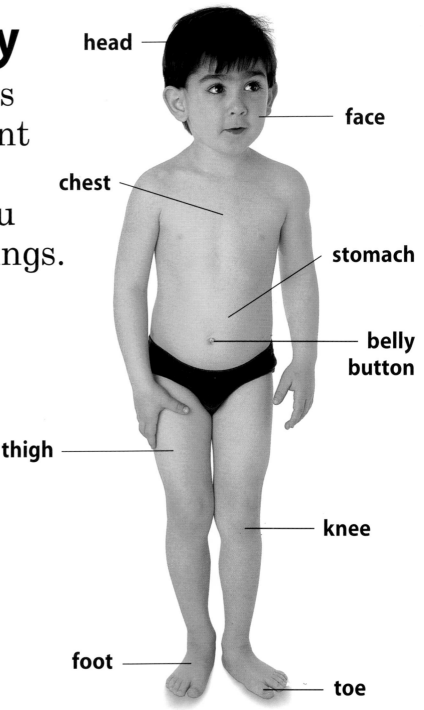

head

face

chest

stomach

belly button

thigh

knee

foot

toe

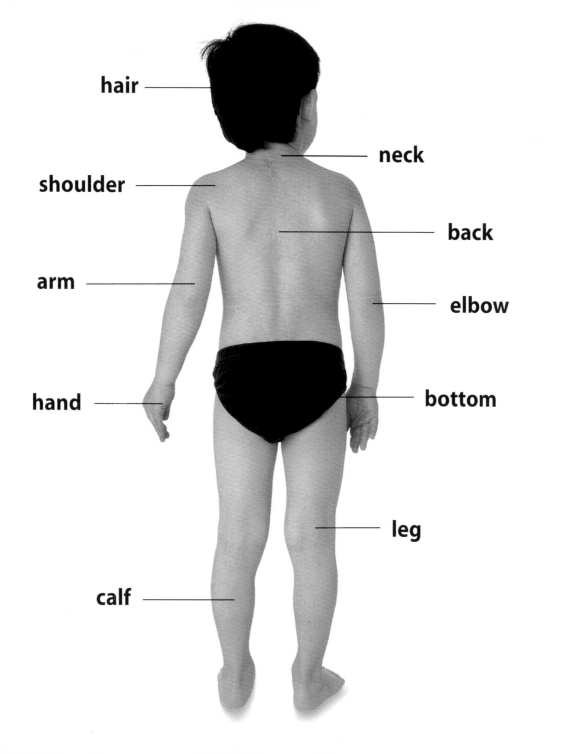

hair

neck

shoulder

back

arm

elbow

hand

bottom

leg

calf

5

Skin and bones

Your body is covered in smooth skin. Inside your body are bones. Your bones join together to make a skeleton.

skull

ribs

hip

knuckles

kneecap

ankle

6

Funny bones

See if you can feel these bones.

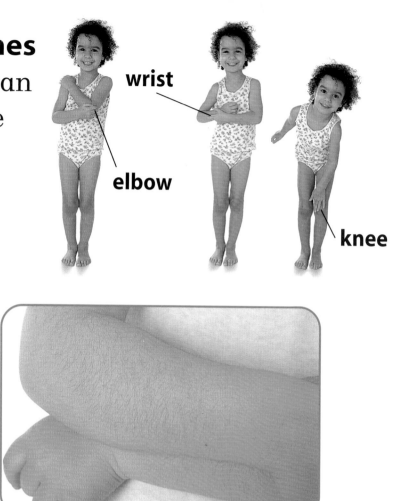

wrist

elbow

knee

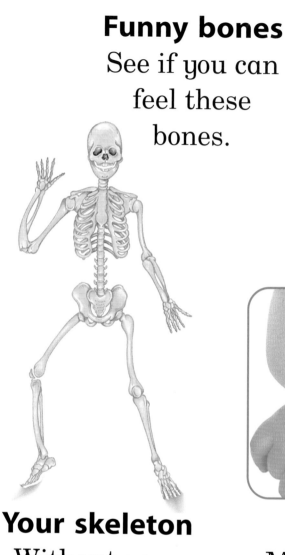

Your skeleton

Without your skeleton, you would be a big blob!

Skin

Most of your skin has short, soft hair on it. Can you feel the hair on your skin?

Mouth

You use your mouth for talking, eating, and smiling!

Talking

You move your tongue and lips to talk.

lips

teeth

tongue

8

Eating

| You use your teeth to take a bite of food. | You use your tongue to taste food. | After chewing your food, you swallow it. |

Smiling
A smile says,
"Hello, it's nice to see you."
Who smiles at you?

Eyes

You use your eyes to see all around you. When you are sad or hurt, tears fall from your eyes.

eyelashes

eyebrow

eyelid

eye

pupil

Eye colors

Eyes can be different colors. What color are your eyes?

gray eyes

Glasses

Glasses can
help you see better.
Do you wear glasses?

Crying

When you cry, your
eyes make salty tears.
Do you cry sometimes?

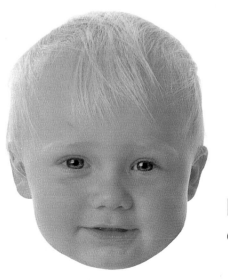

**blue
eyes**

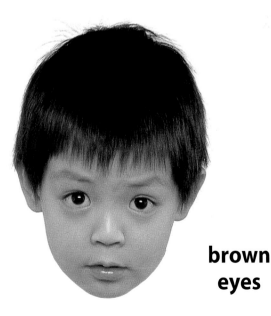

**brown
eyes**

Nose

You use your nose to smell things. You sneeze with your nose, too.

Do these things smell good or bad to you?

perfume

onion

herbs

pasta

nose

nostril

cat food

What do you like to smell?

Ah-Choo!

Sometimes, sneezing
means that you have a cold.
What makes you sneeze?

cat

shark

dog

Animal noses

These animals use their
noses to find food.
How do *you* know when
dinner is ready?

13

Ears

You use your ears to hear all the sounds around you.

Different sounds

What sounds do these things make?

drum

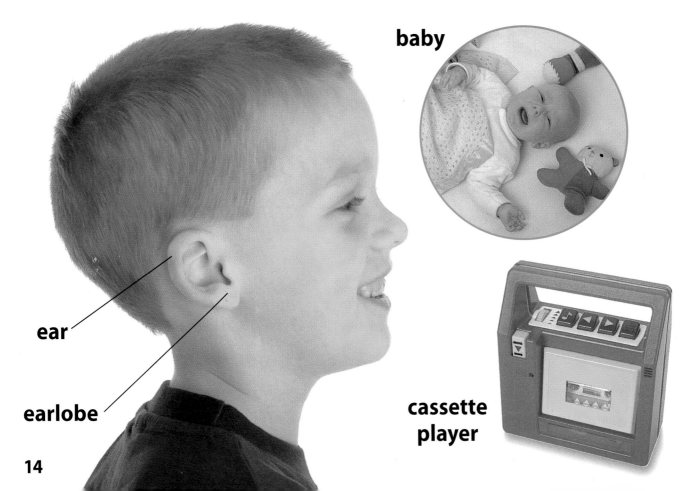

baby

ear

earlobe

cassette player

14

**child in
music class**

bells

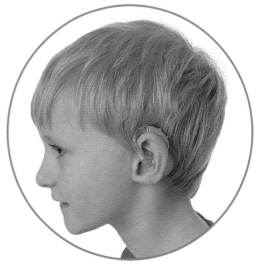

Hearing aid
Some people use
a hearing aid to
help their ears
work better.

Listening
You use
your ears
to listen
to stories.

Do you hear any
sounds right now?

Hands

You use your
hands to hold,
touch, and
feel objects.

Left or right handed?

Do you
draw with
your left
hand or
your right
hand?

finger

nail

knuckle

palm

thumb

wrist

16

Helping hands

Look at all these things your hands help you do. Can you think of some more?

cooking

catching

cutting

making music

painting

Fingerprints

Everybody has different fingerprints. What are yours like?

Arms and legs

You use your arms
and legs to walk,
run, swim, skate,
and play games.

dancing

**skipping
rope**

throwing

Which of these things can you do?

kicking

riding

hopping

19

Animal bodies

Animals have special bodies to help them do different things.

Long tail

A monkey's long tail helps it balance on tree branches.

monkey

Slippery scales

Smooth, slippery scales help a snake slither along the ground.

snake

frog

Feathery wings

A bird could not fly
without its strong,
feathery wings.

Strong legs

A frog's strong back
legs help it jump
high into the air.

seagull

sea lion

Smooth shape

A sea lion's smooth
body and strong tail
help it swim.

Make them match

Can you match the words to the pictures?

smiling

eating

throwing

hopping

cooking

catching

riding

skipping
rope

clapping

hearing

making
music

cutting

bending

23

Glossary/Index

herbs: plants that add flavor to food and are used as a type of medicine. (p. 12)

knuckle: the place in your finger, called a joint, where two of the bones come together. (pp. 6, 16)

nostril: one of the outside openings of your nose. (p. 12)

palm: the inside of your hand. (p. 16)

pupil: the round, dark opening in the center of your eye that lets light in. (p. 10)

skeleton: the arrangement of bones in a body. (pp. 6, 7)

slither: to move by sliding or gliding. (p. 20)

thigh: the top part of your leg, between your hip and your knee. (p. 4)

More Books to Read

Exploring Our Senses (series). Henry Pluckrose (Gareth Stevens)

Join the Total Fitness Gang. Good Health Guides (series). Caroline Glibbery (Gareth Stevens)

Our Bodies. Under the Microscope (series). Casey Horton (Gareth Stevens)

Your Insides. Joanna Cole (Putnam Publishing Group)

Videos

All About Me. (Videotakes)

Me and My Senses. (Phoenix/BFA)

Web Sites

tqjunior.advanced.org/3750/

www.kidshealth.org/kid/index.html

Some web sites stay current longer than others. For further web sites, use your search engines to locate the following topics: *ears, eyes, human body,* and *senses.*